UNIX Shell Programming
Interview Questions
You'll Most Likely Be Asked

Job Interview Questions Series

 **Vibrant Publishers**

www.vibrantpublishers.com

UNIX Shell Programming Interview Questions You'll Most Likely Be Asked

© 2011, By Vibrant Publishers, USA. All rights reserved. No part of this publication may be reproduced or distributed in any form or by any means, or stored in a database or retrieval system, without the prior permission of the publisher.

ISBN-10: 1463689004
ISBN-13: 978-14-63689-00-1

Library of Congress Control Number: 2011911708

This publication is designed to provide accurate and authoritative information in regard to the subject matter covered. The author has made every effort in the preparation of this book to ensure the accuracy of the information. However, information in this book is sold without warranty either expressed or implied. The Author or the Publisher will not be liable for any damages caused or alleged to be caused either directly or indirectly by this book.

Vibrant Publishers books are available at special quantity discount for sales promotions, or for use in corporate training programs. For more information please write to **bulkorders@vibrantpublishers.com**

Please email feedback / corrections (technical, grammatical or spelling) to **spellerrors@vibrantpublishers.com**

To access the complete catalogue of Vibrant Publishers, visit **www.vibrantpublishers.com**

Table of Contents

1. C Shell - Beginner
2. C Shell - Intermediate
3. C Shell - Advanced
4. Bash - Beginner
5. Bash - Intermediate
6. Bash - Advanced
7. HR Questions

This page is intentionally left blank

UNIX Shell Programming Interview Questions

Review these typical interview questions and think about how you would answer them. Read the answers listed; you will find best possible answers along with strategies and suggestions.

This page is intentionally left blank

C Shell - Beginner

1: What must you do before you are able to run your new script for the first time by its name or with an alias?
Answer:
You must make it executable, that is to execute the command:
chmod +x scriptname

2: The following command is included in the .login script of a user:
alias whois ´grep \!ˆ /etc/passwd´
What will be the output, when the user issues the following?
who is guru
Answer:
If there is a defined user account named "guru", or the string guru is contained elsewhere in /etc/passwd file, then the output will be the entry which contains the string "guru", otherwise, it will be an empty line.

3: If the condition *If (-r filename)* fails (returns false), what are the possible reasons?
Answer:
    a) *filename* is not readable by the owner of the process, or,
    b) *filename* does not exist.

4: Which is the difference between the next two statements?
set var = 99
@ var = 99
Answer:
Using the typical assignment form (*set <*), the value assigned in *var* is the string 99. Using the @, the value is the integer 99.

5: Given the code snippet:

@ n = 5
while ($n)
 # actions
<
end

What *actions* should be performed inside the loop, in order to get out of this loop?

Answer:
Any command that changes the value of variable *n*, for it to become 0 sometime. E.g., @ n —

6: What will the output of the following commands be? Explain.
set names = (Kathrin Chris Jacob)
shift names
echo $#names

Answer:
The output will be 2.
shift command gets rid of the first element of the array names. So, the echo command will display 2 as the number of elements of the array.

7: What does the command *rehash* do?

Answer:
rehash recomputes the internal hash table for the PATH variable. If the new command resides in a directory not listed in PATH, add this directory to PATH, and then use *rehash*.

8: How could you ensure that a script will be run in *csh*?

Answer:
The first line of the script could be used to define the shell you want to use, as follows:

#!/bin/csh

This is sufficient to run the script in *csh*.

9: Given that *script1* is an executable C shell script situated in directory */home/myhomedir/project1/data/dir1*, use three ways to run it, explaining the pros and cons.
Answer:
- a) *cd /home/myhomedir/project1/data/dir1/script1*   (You should first cd to the directory path)
- b) */home/myhomedir/project1/data/dir1/script1*   (You should include the absolute directory path)
- c) *script1* (shortest form, but it works only if the directory path is added to the PATH environment variable of the user)

10: What will be the value of the *sixrem* variable, after executing this command?
@ sixrem = $data[2] % 6
Answer:
The expression divides the value of second element of the data array by 6 and assigns the remainder of the division to the *sixrem* variable.

11: Name two ways to obtain the length of a string, giving a simple example for each one.
Answer:
- a) Using the *wc* command:
  set string = "any string"
  @ ln = `echo $string | wc -c` -1
- b) Using the *awk* function *length*:
  set string = "any string"

set ln = `echo $string | awk '{print length($0)}'`

12: Create a script that displays a list of regular files from the current directory.
Answer:
#!/bin/csh -f

foreach i (*)
  if (-f $i) then
    print $i
  endif
end

13: Describe in short the word completion feature of the *tcsh* shell.
Answer:
Completion works anywhere in the command line, not at just the end, for both commands and filenames. Type part of a word and hit the Tab key, and the shell replaces the incomplete word with the complete one in the input buffer. The completion also adds a "/" to the end of completed directories and a space to the end of other words. The shell parses the buffer to determine whether the word you try to complete should be completed as a command, filename or variable. The first word in the buffer and the first word following ';', '|', '|&', '&&' or '||' is considered to be a command. A word beginning with '$' is considered to be a variable. Anything else is a filename. An empty line is 'completed' as a filename.

14: In *tcsh*, how are the remaining choices (if any) listed whenever the word completion fails?

Answer:
They are listed only if the shell variable *autolist* is set.

15: In *tcsh*, how do you disable filename substitution?
Answer:
noglob shell variable can be set to disable this feature.

16: Compare the *sched tcsh* built-in command with the UNIX/Linux *at* command.
Answer:
These commands are similar but not the same. *sched* command runs directly from the shell, so it has access to shell variables and settings. *at* command can run a scheduled command at exactly the specified time.

17: Schedule a prompt change at 10:55 as a reminder for an oncoming event.
Answer:
sched 10:55 set prompt = 'It\'s time for the important meeting: >'

18: What is the impact of *-f* option in the first line of a *csh* script? (#!/bin/csh
versus
#!/bin/csh -f)
Answer:
Using option *-f*, the shell does not load any resource or startup files (.cshrc for a script), or perform any command hashing, and thus starts faster.

19: How can you start a job in the background, and then terminate your login session, without terminating the

background job?
Answer:
Using "no hangup" command, *nohup*:
nohup command > output_file &

20: Which is the difference between
echo c{1,4,2,5,1}
and
echo [c]{1,4,2,5,1} ?
Answer:
The first echo will display *c1 c4 c2 c5 c1*, while the second displays only *c1*.

21: Display the first and last arguments of a script, regardless of the number of arguments, and without a loop.
Answer:
set first = 1
set last = $#argv
echo first argument is $argv[$first]
echo last argument is $argv[$last]

22: Describe the two ways to set the search path in *csh*.
Answer:
setenv PATH /usr/bin:/usr/ucb:/usr/local/bin
setenv PATH ${PATH}:~/bin
The C shell has an alternate way to modify the search path, using a list. Here is the same example as before:
set path = (/usr/bin /usr/ucb /usr/local/bin)
set path = ($path ~/bin)
The variable name is lower case, the syntax is the list form, and a space is used to separate directories.

23: Create a tar archive into /home/user1/myarch.tar, including all files ending in .c, .h, .l, .y, .o and .cc and also the Makefile from two directories, ~/dir1 and ~/dir2.

Answer:

tar cvf /home/user1/myarch.tar ~/{dir1,dir2}/{Makefile,.{c,h,l,o,y,cc}}*

or

tar cvf /home/user1/myarch.tar ~/dir1/Makefile ~/dir1/.[chloy] ~/dir1/*.cc ~/dir2/Makefile ~/dir2/*.[chloy] ~/dir2/*.cc*

24: Your script must be executed with exactly two arguments, otherwise would be terminated. Write a code to implement these checks.

Answer:

if ($#argv <> 2) then
echo "Usage: $0 arg1 arg2"
echo "You must give exactly two parameters"
exit 20
endif

25: Write a pipeline that reads from the j-th line up to the k-th line of a text file, without using *awk*.

Answer:

set total = `cat textfile | wc -l`
set j = 10
set k = 18
@ count = $k - $j
head -$k textfile | tail -$count

C Shell - Intermediate

26: Explain the following commands:
set names = (John Kathrin Chris Jacob)
set names = ($names[1-2] Angela $names[3-])
Answer:
First command creates an array named *names* with the four names as its elements. Second command adds name *Angela* between *Kathrin* and *Chris*.

27: How could you move cursor to specified coordinates on screen? (*tcsh*)
Answer:
echotc cm column row

28: What is the result of this loop?
foreach i ([A-Z]) ? mv $i $i.csh ? end*
Answer:
The loop renames all files that begin with a capital letter, adding the "extension" *.csh*.

29: Assuming there is a label cleanup somewhere in a script, explain the command *onintr cleanup*
Answer:
The script will branch to label *cleanup* if it catches an interrupt signal.

30: Is there a way to repeat a command for a predefined number of times, without using a counter-controlled loop?
Answer:
Using the *repeat* command, e.g.,
repeat 5 ls >> listings

31: *csh* and *tcsh* both support the filename & command completion feature. But the feature works differently in *csh* than in *tcsh*. Name the differences.

Answer:
tcsh automatically completes filenames and commands when the Tab key is hit.
csh does so only when the *filec* variable is set, after the Esc key is hit.

32: Name the special login files for *csh* & *tcsh* in the order used by each shell.

Answer:
A login shell begins by executing commands from the system files */etc/csh.cshrc* and */etc/csh.login*. Then it executes the commands from files in the user's home directory:

a) *~/.cshrc* or *~/.tcshrc*: Executed at each instance of shell startup. *tcsh* executes file *~/.tcshrc if exists,* otherwise uses *~/.cshrc* (if present).

b) *~/.login*: Executed by login shell after *.cshrc* at login.

c) *~/.cshdirs*: Executed by login shell after *.login* (*tcsh*).

33: What do the following lines do? Explain the differences.
ls > filename
ls >! Filename

Answer:
In both forms, the output of *ls* command is redirected to *filename*. If *filename* does not exist, it will be created, otherwise it will be truncated. When the first form is used, if shell parameter *noclobber* is set and *filename* is an existing file, an error results. The '!' in the second form is used to suppress that check.

34: You can run a script by its name, using an alias or using source. Explain the differences in using each of the three methods. When is it suitable to use each method?
Answer:
A script executed by name is not run in current process (a child process is created to run the script), so this method is suitable to be used only if the environment variables and globally defined aliases (in *$HOME/.cshrc*) should be known to the script.

The method that executes a script using an alias is a variant of executing the script by name. In addition, if the alias is defined from shell prompt, it applies only to the current process. To make the alias global, you must define it in *$HOME/.cshrc*, but be careful to keep the number of aliases included there to a relatively small number.

With the third method, the script runs in the current process, thus, any aliases defined in the current process will be known to your script.

35: How could you override a defined alias? Give a simple example.
Answer:
To override an alias, precede the alias with backslash. Fox example, if you have an alias named *rm* which runs a custom script, if you want to run the command *rm* instead of the *rm* alias, you can do it as shown below:

\rm filename

36: You plan to write a script that will process the file passed to it as the only argument on the command line. So, your script must accept at least one argument and this single or first argument must be an existing file. Write the necessary checks,

displaying the appropriate messages.

Answer:

#!/bin/csh
 if ($#argv == 0) then
  echo Error: A file name must be supplied as argument
  exit 10
 else if (! -e $1) then
  echo Error: $1 is not an existing file
  exit 11
 endif
commands to process the file

37: Write a code excerpt that processes (here, just displays) the elements of an array, from the first one to the last one.

Answer:

set myarray = (value1, value2, value3, value4, value5)
set i = 1
while ($#myarray > 0)
  echo "$i array's element is: $myarray[1]"
  shift myarray
  @ i++
end
or,
set myarray = (value1, value2, value3, value4, value5)
set i = 1
foreach val ($myarray[*])
  echo "$i array's element is: $val"
  @ i++
End

38: Complete the last *echo* command with a descriptive message

in the following script. In other words, explain the value of *pct* variable.

#!/bin/csh

set duout = (`du -sk ~`)
@ dir_size = $duout[1]
set dfout = (`df -k | grep /home`)
@ home_size = $dfout[2]
@ pct = $dir_size * 100 / $home_size
echo " <<. $pct ......"

Answer:
echo "Your home directory takes $pct % of /home filesystem"

39: Extract just the mode of a given file, using two different ways.

Answer:
  a) *set file_mode = `ls -l filename | tail -1 | cut -f1 -d" " | cut -c2-`*
  b) *set file_mode = `ls -l filename | awk ' /^-/ {print substr($1,2)}'`*

40: Which is the output of the following excerpt?
netstat -an | awk '/SHED/ {split($4,c,"."); print "Connection to " c[4] " from " $5}' | sort -nt" " -k 3

Answer:
Lines in the format "Connection to *port_number* from *IP_Address*", for each established connection, sorted by *port_number*.

41: Find the position of a substring in a given string. Display a message if the string does not contain this substring.

Answer:
set string = "any string"
set sub = "str"

```
set pos = `echo $string | awk -v s=$sub '{print index($0,s)}'`
if ( $pos == 0 ) then
  echo "$string does not contain the substring $sub"
else
  echo "$sub first occurrence in $string starts in position $pos"
endif
```

42: Change the case of a string.
Answer:

```
set string = "C Shell Programming"
set ustring = `echo $string | awk '{print toupper($0)}'`  # = "C SHELL PROGRAMMING"
set lstring = `echo $string | awk '{print tolower($0)}'`  # = "c shell programming"
```

43: Assume that in a script the value of a variable *limt* becomes equal to 92.1. Display the message:
Upper limit 92.10% in your_system

Answer:

```
set system = `hostname`
printf "Upper limit %f.2%% in the %s" $limt $system
```

44: Suppose a script contains the following snippet:
set fl = /home/dbuser5/reports/fs_report1.txt
echo $fl:e
echo $fl:r
echo $fl:t
echo $fl:h

What do you expect to be displayed?

Answer:

txt

fs_report1
fs_report1.txt
/home/dbuser5/reports

45: Create a script that converts the filenames from current directory to lower case letters.
Answer:
#!/bin/csh -f

foreach file (µlsµ)
  set new file = µecho $file | tr '*AZ]' '[a-z]'`
  if (,$new file` == ,$file`) then
   continue
   endif
   mv $file $new file
end

46: Name some basic differences between *csh* and *tcsh*.
Answer:
tcsh includes a command-line editor, file name and command completion features, and enhanced job control, in comparison with the Berkeley *csh*.

47: Compare the *tcsh* shell variables *correct* and *autocorrect*.
Answer:
autocorrect can be set to correct the word to be completed before any completion attempt. *correct* can be set to '*cmd*' to correct command names or to '*all*' to correct the entire line, each time return is hit.

48: What is the purpose of the special alias *shell*?

Answer:
The *shell* special alias can be set to specify an interpreter other than the shell itself.

49: Which is the method to bind the keys to the standard *vi* or *emacs* bindings?
Answer:
Shell's built-in command *bindkey*. Its *-e* option binds all keys to standard *emacs* bindings, while *-v* option binds to standard *vi* bindings.

50: Which is the purpose of shell's variable *color*?
Answer:
If set, it enables color display for the builtin *ls-F* and it passes *--color=auto* to *ls*.

51: Set your prompt to display *username@hostname: pwd>*
Answer:
set prompt = "%n@%m: %/ >"

52: How can you start (from shell prompt) 2 commands "in the background", ensuring that the second command will start after the completion of the first one?
Answer:
(command 1 ; command 2) &

53: Write a script to display a sorted listing of the unique words in a text file.
Answer:
#!/bin/csh

set txt_file = text_file_name
tr -s ' ' < $txt_file | tr ' ' '\n' | sort | uniq

54: Display the value of your PATH variable with each path in a separate line.
Answer:
echo $PATH | tr ':' ' \n' | sort

55: Why the inclusion of a dot (.) in a search path is not a good practice?
Answer:
The current working directory may be a world writable directory (like /tmp). World writable directories must not be included in the PATH variable due to security reasons. It may also cause problems in the execution of commands, if the current directory contains executable files - the names of which match reserved words (standard commands, etc).

56: Explain the logical expression @ x = ($n < 5 || 20 <= $n) and then also write the negation of this expression.
Answer:
variable x is 0 (false) when n lies between 5 and 19 inclusive, but is 1 (true) otherwise.
The following variable y is the negation of x.
@ y = (!($n < 5 || 20 <= $n))
The parentheses surrounding the logical expressions are needed when an expression contains >, <, |, or &.

57: Are there any differences between the next two commands? When is it suitable to use each one?
csh -x myscript

csh -v myscript
Answer:
The *-x* option echoes the command lines after variable substitution, while the -v option echoes the command lines before variable substitution.

The *-v* option is normally used to identify the line at which the script is failing, while the -x option is normally used to locate errors in variable substitution.

Both these options can produce lots of output, so it is often sensible to redirect the output to a file, to be examined at a comfortable pace.

58: The creation of aliases in your *.cshrc* file does have a drawback: if you define many aliases in the *.cshrc* file, it will decelerate process activation. What would be a possible work around?
Answer:
One possible work around is to define a few aliases that run other scripts, each of which in turn define many related aliases. Thus you only create the definitions when they are required.

59: Explain this small script:
#!/bin/csh
foreach dfile (/home/users/project1/*)
　if (-z $dfile || $dfile == "core") then
　　rm $dfile
　endif
end
Answer:
This script will delete zero length files and dumped core files from the specified directory.

60: A script prompts the user to type in something, using the following syntax:

echo -n "Enter some input ->"
set IN = $<

What would happen if the user had typed? *A B C D E*
Correct your syntax to avoid the possible problems.

Answer:

The shell replaces the *$<* with the user input, that is:

set IN = A B C D E

and then executes that command. This set command, however, will assign the value A to the IN variable, a C to the B variable, an E to the D variable, so after the execution of the above command, in the script there will be 3 variables, instead of one (IN).

The solution is to use *$<* in quotes (double):

set IN = "$<"

Thus, when the user inputs the string A B C D E, the shell will have the following command to execute:

set IN = "A B C D E"

and it will assign the quoted string to the IN variable.

C Shell - Advanced

61: Fix the next switch statement, explaining your corrections:

```
switch ($argv[$i])
  case quit:   breaksw
  case list:   ls
   breaksw
  case delete:
  case erase:
   @ k = $i
   rm $argv[$k]
   breaksw
endsw
```

Answer:

```
switch ($argv[$i])
  case quit:
   breaksw   # the commands for a particular case
      # MUST NOT be on the same line
  case list:
   ls           # same as above
   breaksw
  case delete:
  case erase:
   @ k = $i + 1 # the value of $argv[$i] here is "erase"
    # a logical syntax would be script erase filename,
    # in order to erase the second argument.
   rm $argv[$k]
   breaksw
endsw
```

62: Name some basic differences between bash and *csh* syntax and/or features.

Answer:

a) Bash shell has functions, C shell does not have.
b) Bash shell assigns values to variables using the assign operator (*variable=value*); C shell uses *set* command (*set variable = value*)
c) Bash shell has more advanced command substitution than C shell.
d) Bash shell has advanced file handling mechanisms; *csh* itself has no file handling capabilities.

63: Suggest a way to overcome lack of functions in C shells.
Answer:
A way to overcome lack of functions is using a "clever" combination of alias and scripts. E.g.:
alias holder ' source ~$USER/.tsch/holder_func'
where the script *holder_func* contains the code to execute.

64: From /tmp directory, issue (cd ; pwd) ; pwd. Explain the performed actions and the output.
Answer:
cd returns user to his home directory, so the first *pwd* displays the home directory. But, since parenthesized commands are always executed in a subshell, second *pwd* displays /tmp, leaving the user where he was.

65: Write a code excerpt that prompts for a filename, reads the user input, checks if this is a regular file and if so, stores it in an array for further processing. The procedure must be repeated until the user hits the Enter key.
Answer:
#!/bin/csh
set i = 1

```
set fl = anything
while ( $fl )
 echo -n "Give a filename ->"
 set fl  = $<
 if ( $fl  = "" ) then
  break
 endif
 if ( ! -f $fl ) then
  continue
 endif
 set  $files[$i] = $fl
 @ i++
end
echo "Number of files: $#files"
echo "Files are: $files[*]"
```

66: Use *awk* mathematical functions to calculate the area of a circle (area = PI*rad^2)

Answer:

```
alias mathcalc ' awk "BEGIN{ print \!* }" '

set rad = 1.3
set circle_area = `mathcalc atan2(0,-1)*${rad}*${rad}`
```

Explanation: The *alias* defines a kind of mathematical calculator called *mathcalc*, which uses the "one-liner" *awk* to perform calculations (limited to the set of mathematical functions available in *awk*). Then, this calculator is used to calculate the circle's area. It uses the arctangent function *atan2* that evaluates PI.

67: Use *awk* in order to split an entry from /etc/passwd file into

an array, replacing the password field with the string "secret".
Answer:
set user = username
set entry = `grep ^$user: /etc/passwd | awk ' {$2 = "secret"; split($0,a,":"); for (i=1; i<=7; i++) print a[i]}'`

68: Explain the following snippet:
set ports = (`netstat -an | awk '/SHED/ {split($4,c,"."); print c[4]}'`)
set remaddrs = (`netstat -an | awk '/SHED/ print $5}'`)
@ i = 1
foreach port ($ports[*])
  set service = `grep $port /etc/services | cut -f1 -d' '`
  echo "$service connection established from $remaddrs[$i]"
  @ i++
end

Answer:
It creates an array that holds the port numbers used for each established network connection and a second array that holds the corresponding remote IP Addresses. Then, using a *foreach* loop, "resolves" the port numbers to service names, and displays a descriptive message in the form "Service_name connection established from Remote_IP_Address" for each connection.

69: Name the available ways (with examples) to replace any occurrence of a substring with another substring in a string.
Answer:
    a) Using *sed*:
        set sedstring = `echo $text | sed 's/search_string/replacement/g'`
    b) Using *awk*:

set awkstring = `echo $string | awk -v s1="$search" -v s2="$substitute" '{gsub(s1,s2); print $0}'`
c) Using editing modifiers: (limited use)
set text = "now is the time for all good men"
echo $text:gs/o/O/

70: Write a snippet to categorize the files from a directory, based on their extension (for simplicity, take care only for .c, .o, .txt, and .png files). Create an array for each extension, containing the filenames. Finally, display the number of files for each extension.
Answer:
#!/bin/csh

```
set dir = /home/~       # the directory path
foreach fl ($dir/*)
  switch ($fl)
    case *.c:
    set cfiles = ($cfiles[*] $fl)
    breaksw
    case *.o:
    set ofiles = (ofiles[*] $fl)
    breaksw
    case *.txt:
    set txtfiles = (txtfiles[*] $fl)
    breaksw
    case *.png:
    set pngfiles = (pngfiles[*] $fl)
    breaksw
    default:
    breaksw
```

endsw

end

echo "There are $#cfiles .c files, $#ofiles .o files, $#txtfiles txt files and $#pngfiles .png files in directory $dir"

71: Write a script that will display a menu of choices to the user. The menu should be displayed over and over, until the user will select the specific "exit" option. The script should give to the user the following options:
    a)   rename a file
    b)   display the contents of the file
    c)   display the first and the last line of the file
    d)   exit (or quit) the script

All the four choices (except exit) will ask for a filename and the script should check if that file exists or not. Is it possible to create a function to achieve this purpose?

Answer:

No, there is no safe way to return a variable's value, if it is defined in a child script, to its parent. The script goes as follows:

#!/bin/csh -f

set ans = 0
while ($ans != 4)
echo "   MENU"
echo "=================="
echo "1   Rename a file"
echo "2   View a file's contents"
echo "3   Examine 1rst and last lines of a file"
echo "4   Quit - number 4 is the only acceptable choice"
echo ""
echo "Make your choice ->"

```
set ans = $<

switch ($ans)
  case   [1Rr]:
  echo "Enter a filename ->"
  set fl = $<
  if ( ! -f "$fl" ) then
   echo (You must enter an existing file/ try again<(
   breaksw
  endif
  mv  $fl ${fl}.bak
  echo "Moving $fl to ${fl}.bak"
  breaksw
  case  [2Vv]:
  echo "Enter a filename ->"
  set fl = $<
  if ( ! -f "$fl" ) then
   echo (You must enter an existing file/ try again<(
   breaksw
  endif
  cat $fl
  breaksw
  case  [3Ee]:
  echo "Enter a filename ->"
  set fl = $<
  if ( ! -f "$fl" ) then
   echo (You must enter an existing file/ try again<(
   breaksw
  endif
  echo "First line:"
  head -1 $fl
```

```
        echo "Last line:"
        tail -1 $fl
        breaksw
      case 4:
        exit
      default:
        echo "Only valid choices are the displayed numbers or the first letter of each choice, except the last one"
        breaksw
    endsw
end
```

72: Create a script that will be run automatically when the user logs into the system, and send a mail message to the user, if the total number of aliases on his .cshrc file are greater than a threshold (let's say 40).

Answer:

```
#!/bin/csh -f

set thres = 40
set total = `grep ^alias $HOME/.cshrc | wc -l`
if ($ total > $ thres ) then
   mail -s "Too many aliases on your login scripts!!" $USER << EOF
   Dear user $USER
   WARNING:  Your defined aliases on your .cshrc are more than the allowed upper limit ($thres)
   Please do the necessary changes to lower their number.
   System Administrator
   EOF
Endif
```

73: Display the filenames and permissions of each file in your current directory.
Answer:
set files = (`ls -l | grep -v ^total | tr -s ' ' | cut -f9 -d' '`)
set perms = (`ls -l | grep -v ^total | tr -s ' ' | cut -f1 -d' ' | cut -c2-`)
echo "   FILE PERMISSIONS LIST "
echo "   ===================="
set tot = $#files[*]
set count = 1
foreach fl ($files[*])
  echo "$fl \t $perms[$count]"
  @ count++
End

74: Create a script that creates a list of all file systems (mount points) on the current system and the current percent used.
Answer:
set fs = (`df | grep -v ^Filesystem | tr -s ' ' | cut -f5 -d' '`)
set pcts = (`df | grep -v ^Filesystem | tr -s ' ' | cut -f4 -d' '`)
set count = $#fs[*]
set i = 1
while ($i <= $count)
  echo "File system $fs[$i] is $pct[$i} used"
  @ i++
End

75: Explain the following script and suggest any enhancements:

if (-z "$1")
then

```
    echo "Usage: `basename $0` filename"
    exit 20
fi

Username=guru
pword=/home/guru/password.file
Password=`cat $pword`
Filename=`basename $1`

Server="Servername"
Directory="dirpath"

ftp -n $Server <<EOF
user $Username $Password
binary
bell
cd $Directory
put $Filename
bye
EOF
exit 0
```

Answer:

The script checks if there is one argument in the command line. It starts an ftp session to a server, and using a *here document*, passes to it some ftp commands: username and password for that user, which is read from a file. During the session, it changes the directory and transfers a file to the remote server.

Suggestions: Security is the most important point with this script. It uses ftp (it would be better to use a secure equivalent, like *sftp*), and the password is stored in a text file in plain text!!!! It would be better to use the available encryption / decryption tools (like the standard *crypt* function).

The other point is the flexibility: All parameters are hard coded into the script. It would be better to ask them from the user during script's execution.

76: Assuming that script *myscript.csh* executes successfully, explain why the command:
if ({ myscript.csh }) echo my program worked
will work, while the command:
if (myscript.csh) echo my program did not work
will not.
Also name a case in which neither the first syntax will work nor the second.
Answer:
Zero is true in the exit status, while non-zero is true in expressions. In other words/ in the exit status "true" means zero (0)/ while in expressions "true" means any non-zero value. Thus, if "myscript.*csh*" executes successfully/ it has an exit value of "true"/ that is zero (0). But using it in an expression like the above (if (myscript.*csh*) ...)/ a zero value means "false". There is a way to get the exit status inside an expression as it is. It's not a common technique, however. The solution is to enclose the command inside curly braces. If the command within curly braces is successful (status of zero), then the expression is 1, or true. Thus, the expression if ({ myscript.*csh* }) evaluates as true, if the myscript.*csh* executes successfully.

However, if you try to redirect standard output, it will not work:
if ({ grep pattern file >/dev/null }) echo found pattern

77: In which case the following command would be useful?
if (Z$argv[1] =~ Z-r) echo option '-r'

Answer:

The script will accept a "-r" option. However, the following test will not work:

if ($argv[1] =~ -r) echo something

If the first argument is "-r", then this is evaluated as:

if (-r =~ -r) echo something

The C shell will assume you meant to use a file operator, and test the file "=~" to see if it is readable. Then it sees the next operator, which is again a "-r," but in this case there is no filename afterwards. This generates a syntax error. The solution is to place a dummy character (like Z here) before both strings.

78: Use the *bc* calculator in order to do a variable comparison involving floating-point numbers. Write your example as part of an *if* conditional statement.

Answer:

set var1 = 0.4
if (`echo "if ( ${var1} <= 1.1 ) 1" | bc`) then
   <statements when $var1 is less than or equal to 1.1>
Endif

79: Write a *while* loop using a floating-point comparison statement as the loop condition (and loop control).

Answer:

*set curvalue = 1.678*10^03*
set upper = 1289.56
while (`echo "if ( $curvalue <= $upper) 1" | bc`)
  <statements when $curvalue <= 1289.56>
End

80: There is no simple file reading facility in the C-shell. What

could you use to tide this over?
Answer:
A combination of *awk* and shell loops is a work around.

81: Extract the n-th line of a text file and assign it in a variable.
Answer:
set text = `awk -v ln=$j '{if (NR==ln) print $0}' textfile`
where variable *j* define the n-th line.

82: Assuming that input_file is a text file with space-separated fields, what will be the value of *ncol* when the next command will be executed?
set ncol = `awk '{if (FNR==1) print NF}' input_file`
Answer:
The value of *ncol* will be equal to the number of fields in the first line of this file.
FNR is a built-in variable in *awk*, the value of which is the number of the records read. NF is another *awk* variable, the value of which is the number of fields in that record (by default, space-separated).

83: Find the minimum of the integer numbers that are stored in an array.
Answer:
set array = (4, -2, 5, 8, 13, 1)
set array_org = ($array[*])   # create a clone, to preserve the original numbers
set min = $array[1]
while ($#array > 0)   # if there is at least one element
  if ($min > $array[1]) then
    set min = $array[1]
  endif

shift array   # discards the first element of the array
end

echo "The original numbers are: $array_org[*]"
echo "The minimum number is: $min"

84: Explain the following block of commands:
foreach luser (`who | cut -f1 -d' ' | uniq`)
  if (-f /allfiles/$luser.msg) then
  mail $luser < $luser.msg
  echo "Message sent to $luser"
  else
  mail $luser << END
  Dear $luser,
  No message file has been created for you.
  Please check your settings
  END
  endif
end

Answer:
The *luser* variable takes as value the username of each logged in user in the system (unique names, if some users have more than one login sessions). Inside the loop it checks if a "personalized" message file exists for each user, which is named in the format *"username.msg"*. If so, it sends that file to the user mailbox. If not, creates a message using the *"here document"* and it sends it to the user, informing him about the nonexistence of the file he is waiting for.

85: The C shell provides one way to read a line:
set VAR = $<

Which is the limitation of this syntax?
Answer:
This command always reads from standard input. $<$ is only STDIN, and cannot change for the duration of the script.

86: Explain the following snippet:
foreach line ("`cat /etc/passwd`")
  set line = "$line:gas/ /_/"
  set line = "$line:gas/:/ /"
  set argv = ($line)
  set name1 = $1
  set name2 = "$5:gas/_/ /"
  echo $name2
end

Answer:
It is a possible workaround in order to read a file line by line. In each loop iteration, the line variable takes the next line from the /etc/passwd file (note the double quotes around the `cat /etc/passwd`), and then, using variable modifiers, the script replaces first the spaces with underscores and then the : with spaces. Then it sets the positional parameters to the fields of the line, it replaces again the underscores with a space, and displays the comments field.

87: Fix any syntax or logical error in the following script:
 # This script creates a list of the subdirectories in a path
#!/bin/csh

echo "Subdirectories in $DirPath"
cd $DirPath
foreach file (*)

```
if ( -e $file ) then
 echo $file
 endif
end
```
Answer:
a) The line *#!/bin/csh* must be the FIRST in the script.
b) The *DirPath* variable is not set, so, the *cd $DirPath* command changes to the user's home directory (*cd*).
c) The test (*-e $file*) checks if the value of file variable exists, not if it is a directory. It must be: (*-d "$file"*).
d) It is safer to use double quotes around the variable substitution expressions, e.g. *"$file"*.

The correct script is:
#!/bin/csh
 # This script creates a list of the subdirectories in a path
set DirPath = "/home/user1/mydir"
echo "Subdirectories in $DirPath"
cd "$DirPath"
foreach file (*)

```
if ( -d "$file" ) then
 echo "$file"
 endif
end
```

88: Explain this script:
#!/bin/csh

echo "FILES   # LINES   SIZE"
cd
foreach FL (*)

```
if ( -f "$FL" ) then
  set count = `cat "$FL" | wc -l`
  set size = `ls -l "$FL" | tr -s ' ' | cut -f5 -d' '`
  echo "$FL            $count           $size"
endif
end
```

Answer:

This script creates a report for all regular files in user's home directory, displaying the name of the file (1st column), the number of lines contained into the file (2nd column) and its size (3rd column).

89: Are there any differences between the next two commands?

```
set lines = `cat filename | wc -l`
set lines = ( `wc -l filename` )
```

Answer:

In the first command, the output is just the lines count (only the number), while in the second one the output is the lines count and the filename (that is why the parentheses are necessary).
In the first statement, the used cat command decelerates the execution, so it will be slower than the second one.

90: Explain the following code block:

```
set string = "This is a string that contains the substring str 3 times"
set sub = "str"
set pos = (1)
set origstr = "$string"
while ( $pos[1] > 0 )
  set pos = `echo $string | awk -v s=$sub '{ps = index($0,s); print ps, substr($0,ps)}'`
```

```
    if ( $pos[1] > 0 ) then
     set positions = ($positions[*] $pos[1])
     set string = "$pos[2-]"
    endif
  end
```

```
echo "Substring $sub found in $#positions:"
echo $positions[*]
```

Answer:

It uses the *awk* functions *index* and *substr* in combination with a *while* loop in order to find every occurrence of a given substring in a string and displays the positions of them. Each time inside the loop the *awk* returns as a pair of one position and the remaining substring, and this pair is stored in an array. In the next iteration of the loop, the previously extracted substring is used, until the *awk* function *index* returns 0, meaning that the substring could not be located.

91: Suppose that you have a contacts file in the format (no headers line):
Name, Surname, Street, City, State, email, Telephone
Explain the following excerpt:
#!/bin/csh

```
foreach record ("`cat contacts`")
  set record = "$record:gas/ /_/"
  set record = "$record:gas/\,/ /"
  set argv = "$record"
  set name = "$1:gas/_/ /"
  set surname = "$2:gas/_/ /"
  set street = "$3:gas/_/ /"
```

```
    set city = "$4:gas/_/ /"
    set state = "$5"
    set email = "$6:gas/_/ /"
    set tel = "$7:gas/_/ /"
    echo "RR   Name: $2 $1" >> ${5}.contacts
    echo "              $3 $4" >> ${5}.contacts
    echo "              $6  " >> ${5}.contacts
    echo "              $7  " >> ${5}.contacts
end
```

Answer:

This script creates one contacts file of each state, named *state.contacts*. It processes the original contacts file, line by line, replacing the spaces with underscores and then the commas with spaces. Then it sets the positional parameters to the fields of each line, sets 7 variables (one for each field), and echoes these variables in 4 lines, appending them to the appropriate file for that state.

92: Which is the valid syntax of *getopt* command in a C shell?

Answer:

```
set argv=`getopt OptionString $*`
```

93: Explain in short the following script:

```
#!/bin/csh


set OUTPUT_FILE=""
set DO_LONG=""
set argv="`getopt "hlo:" $*`"
if ( $status != 0 ) then
  echo "Usage: $0 [-l] [-o outputfile] [path ...]"
  exit 1
```

endif
while ("$1" != "--")
  switch($1)
   case "-h":
   echo "Usage: $0 [-l] [-o outputfile] [path ...]"
   exit 1
   case "-o":
   set OUTPUT_FILE="$2"
   shift
   breaksw
   case "-l":
   set DO_LONG="-l"
   breaksw
  endsw
  shift
end
shift
if ("$OUTPUT_FILE" == "") then
  ls $DO_LONG $*
else
  ls $DO_LONG $* > $OUTPUT_FILE
endif

Answer:

This script uses *getopt* command that processes the entire argument list at once. If the argument list matches, *getopt* canonicalizes (reorders in the typical way used by UNIX commands) the argument list, putting the flags and their optional arguments prior to any non-flag arguments, adding a single trailing "--" argument to indicate that there are no more flags to process.

In case of *-h* option, the script displays a "usage" message and terminates.

In case of -o option, the script sets the OUTPUT_FILE variable to the argument that follows. In case of -l option, the script sets the DO_LONG variable to -l. The shift command that follows the while loop removes trailing --.

The script runs ls $* (where $* are the remaining arguments), if no option was used; it runs ls -l $* command, if -l option was used and ls -l $* command, redirecting the output to OUTPUT_FILE file, if -o file was used.

94: Write a script which calculates the min, max and average of a set of floating-point numbers, stored in an array.
Answer:

```
set array = (5, 10, 2, 13, 0.2345)
foreach num ($array[*])
  echo $num >> nums_file
end
awk '{if(min==`'`(){min=max=$1}; if($1=max) {max=$1}; if($1< min)
{min=$1}; total+=$1; count+=1} END {print "Average is: "total/count,
(Min is: (min/ (Max is: (max}' nums_file
```

95: You have an input data file with a symmetrical schema (the same number of fields in each record) where the first line contains the headings of the fields. You want to extract the 3rd column (field) of the actual data records, that is, of each record except the headers line (1st line) and any comment lines (assume that they begin with # or *). Give a solution and explain it in short.
Answer:

```
set cn = 3
set ncols = `awk '{FNR == 1 {print NF}' input_file `
```

```
if ( $cn <= $ncols ) then
  set col$cn = `awk -v i=$cn '$0 !~ /^[#*]/ && FNR != 1 { print $i }'
input_file `
else
  echo "The column number must be in the range 1 to $ncols"
endif
```

The variable *ncols* contains the total number of columns in each record. The *if* structure is used to avoid the case where the position number of the requested column is greater than the total number of columns. *col3* will be an array of the values of the third column.

96: Suppose that input_file is a tabular data file with an asymmetric schema, that is, each record (line) may have different number of fields, and that the first 3 lines describe the used schema. Explain the following excerpt:

```
set cn = 3
set ccounts = `awk '{FNR > 3 {print NF}' input_file `
set ccounts1 = ( $ccounts[*] )
set ccounts2 = ( $ccounts[*] )
set mincn = $ccounts[1]
while ( $ccounts1 > 0 )
  if ( $mincn > $ccounts1[1] ) then
   set mincn = $ccounts1[1]
   endif
   shift ccounts1
end
set maxcn = $ccounts2[1]
while ( $ccounts2 > 0 )
  if ( $maxcn < $ccounts2[1] ) then
```

```
    set maxcn = $ccounts2[1]
  endif
  shift ccounts2
end


if ( $cn <= $maxcn ) then
  set col$cn = ` awk -v i=$cn  -v minc=$mincn 'FNR > 3 { (FN < minc ) ? print FN "null" : print $i }' input_file `
else
  echo "The column number must be in the range $mincn to $maxcn"
endif
```

Answer:

This script extracts the content of a column from an asymmetric data file:

The *cn* variable holds the column to be extracted. The *ccounts* array holds the number of fields of all actual data records (FNR > 3). The arrays *ccounts1* and *ccounts2* are duplicates of the *ccount* array, used to calculate the minimum and maximum numbers from the array *ccounts*. We use these temporary arrays in order to preserve the original array to use it later. The first *while* loop calculates the minimum value and the second the maximum value. A *shift* command in each loop iteration, discards the first element of the array. The *if* statement then checks if the number of the requested column (field) is less than the maximum number, and if so, the *awk* command prints the content of this column if there are any (FN >= *minc*), or the string "FNnull", otherwise. If the number of the requested column is greater than the maximum number, the script displays a message.

**97: Suppose you have a data file but its internal format does not remain consistent. You want to extract two columns from this file, but you don't know the order of the columns, only their headers: Name, and email.
Write the script that will achieve these tasks.
Answer:**
#!/bin/csh -f

set fl = filename
set namepos = `head -1 "$fl" | awk '{split($0,a) ; for ( j in a ) { if (a[j] = "Name") {print j}}}' `
set mailpos = `head -1 "$fl" | awk '{split($0,a) ; for ( j in a ) { if (a[j] = "email") {print j}}}' `
foreach line ("`cat $fl`")
  set line = "$line:gas/ /_/"
  set argv = "$line"
  set name = "$argv[$namepos]"
  set name = "$name:gas/_/ /"
  set names = ($names[*] "$name")
  set mail = "$argv[$mailpos]"
  set mails = ($mails[*] "$mail")
end

**98: Create a script to read a textfile line by line, to the end of the file. Do not use *awk*.
Answer:**
set inputfile = textfile
set total = `cat $inputfile | wc -l`
@ count = 1

while ($count <= $total)

```
if ($count == 1 )
then
 set record = "`head $count $inputfile`"
 @ count++
else
 set record = "`head -$count $inputfile | tail -$1`"
 @ count++
endif
<more commands to process the record>
End
```

99: Which is a limitation in options handling in C shells?
Answer:
There is not an equivalent to *getopts* bash built-in in C shells. The only way to handle command line options is the command *getopt*. This command processes the entire arguments list at once and because of the way it reconstructs the arguments list (adds a simple trailing "--" argument), it does not support arguments with spaces. (The GNU -Linux version of *getopt* provides flags that cause it to output a string quoted for a shell to work around this limitation, but this is not portable).

100: Rewrite the next script, using a more readable and clear logic:
#!/bin/csh

```
@ num = 0
echo "Enter a number between 0 and 223"
set num $<
if ( $num > 0 && $num <= 223 )
then
```

```
if ( $num < 127 )
then
 echo "Number may be first octet for class-A network IP"
else
 if ( $num > 127 && $num <= 191 )
 then
  echo "Number may be first octet for class-B network IP"
 else
  if ( $num == 127 )
  then
   echo "Number is used for loopback"
  else
   echo "Number may be first octet for class-C network IP"
  endif
 endif
endif
else
 echo "number is not usable for first octet in an IP address"
endif
```

Answer:
```
#!/bin/csh

@ num = 0
echo "Enter a number betwwen 0 and 223"
set num $<
if ( $num <= 0 || $num > 223 )
then
 echo "number is not usable for first octet in an IP address"
 exit
endif
```

```
if ( $num == 127 )
then
  echo "Number is used for loopback"
  exit
endif

if ( $num < 127 )
then
  echo "Number may be first octet for class-A network IP"
  exit
endif

if ($num <= 191)
then
  echo "Number may be first octet for class-B network IP"
else
  echo "Number may be first octet for class-C network IP"
endif
```

It is easier for someone to follow this solution, but the order is important for the 4 *if* statements in this case. Note also the *exit* command in the first 3 *if* statements.

Bash - Beginner

101: Consider the following message:
"bash: scriptfile: Execute permission denied."
How could you fix it (assuming that you are the owner of scriptfile)?
Answer:
The user does not have execute permission on *scriptfile*.
We could run the following command to grant execute permission for everybody:
chmod +x scriptfile

102: The *case* statement is useful for comparing the value of a variable against a list of possible matches. True or false?
Answer:
TRUE

103: You don't remember the correct option (switch) for *sort* command, in order to sort some entries in reverse order. What could you do?
Answer:
Open the man page for *sort* command, run the command:
man sort
and then search the keyword "reverse" (the search starts using the /).

104: The first line of a shell script is:
#!/bin/bash
How does the shell interpret this line?
Answer:
The *exec* system call which is invoked to start a script, will check the first two bytes of the script for a special sequence, #!, which specifies the interpreter executable to be used for executing this

script, on the same line .

105: You need to find all files under your /home directory that were not accessed during last 10 days. What could you do?
Answer:
Run the following command:
find /home -type f -atime +10

106: How could you check if there are running *sshd* processes on your system?
Answer:
We could check by running the command:
ps - ef | grep sshd
or
pgrep sshd

107: What happens when you run the following command?
mkdir -p /tmp/{my,your,his,her}dir/{contacts,files}
  a) 6 new directories will be created under the /tmp
  b) 8 new directories will be created under the /tmp directory
  c) 2 new directories will be created under the /tmp directory
  d) It will not create new directories and an error message will be displayed.

Answer:
Option b) is correct. 8 new directories will be created.

108: The next line is the beginning of a conditional statement in a *Bash* script:
if [[$1 = $var1 || = $var2]]

This statement has at least an error. Identify and correct it.

Answer:

There is a syntax error in *test* condition. In the second expression, there is no left part. Also, it is better to use double quotes around the variable substitution's expressions used in *test*, to ensure that syntax errors will not arise in case a variable is null or undefined. The correct statement is:

if [["$1" = "$var1" || "$1" = "$var2"]]

109: A *for* loop requires an arguments list. This list can result from:

- a) a) Command substitution: *for var in $(command) <.*
- b) Variable substitution: *for var in $anothervar <.*
- c) c) Arguments given in the command line: *for var in $* <.*
- d) d) A test condition: *for var in [["$var" -eq 3]] ....*
- e) All the above

Answer:

Options a), b) as well as c) will give the desired result.

110: Given the following nested loops, which command would you use in place of command-to-process-file for the shell to execute the last cat command, if the test condition is met?

while true
do
  while true
  do
  echo "Please enter a filename:-->\c"
  read ans
  if [[-f "$ans"]]

```
    then
     command-to-process-file
    fi
   done
  done
cat $ans
```

Answer:
break 2

111: What would happen if the following command was in the .bash_profile of a user?
trap ' ' INT
Answer:
The user could not interrupt any command started from that shell. The *trap* command would trap the INT signal, changing the behavior of the shell to ignore that signal.

112: The value of a variable should be compared against 8 possible values (and/or patterns) and some commands, different for each possible value, should be run. Which is the structure that you would prefer for these checks?
Answer:
case "$var" in
pattern_1) <.
;;
<.
;;
pattern_8) <.
;;
Esac

113: What is the expected output from the following command?
echo {a .. z}
Answer:
It echoes all alphabetic lowercase characters, that is, a b c d e f g h j k l m n o p q r s t u v w x y z

114: How can you run a job in the background?
Answer:
Add the & in the end of the command line, that is, *command &*

115: What is the action performed by the command *cd -*?
Answer:
It changes the current working directory to the previous working directory. It is equivalent to *cd $OLDPWD*.

116: Which are the special meanings of character ~ for the bash shell?
Answer:
    a) the ~ is equivalent to *$HOME*, that is, to the home directory of the user.
    b) ~dbuser1 corresponds to the home directory of user dbuser1, if there is such a user; otherwise, it is treated as the literal string ~dbuser1.
    c) ~+ means the current working directory, so it is equivalent to *$PWD*.
    d) ~- means the previous working directory, so it is equivalent to $OLDPWD.
    e) =~ is a regular expression match.

117: Which is the difference between *variable5* and *$variable5*?
Answer:

variable5 is the name of a variable, and *$variable5* is a reference to the value of this variable.

118: What is defined with the command *variable=value*, a local or an environment variable?
Answer:
A local variable is defined.

119: How can you find the bash shell version which is installed on your system?
Answer:
echo $BASH_VERSION
For more details, use the array *BASH_VERSINFO*.

120: What does the bash built-in variable *EDITOR* do?
Answer:
It invokes the default editor, usually *vi* or *emacs*.

121: What is the purpose of shell built-in variable *PATH*?
Answer:
To define a list of paths to executables, *PATH* will be used by shell to find those files by their relative names.

122: Is there any way to declare an integer variable in bash?
Answer:
Yes, the *typeset -i* command (or the equivalent *declare*).

123: How would the shell interpret the command "*echo ??a*"?
Answer:
Before starting the execution of echo, the shell will replace the 2 *??*. For the shell, the ? represents any one character in a filename.

But the first dot in a filename cannot be substituted by any character and should be given literally. This command would output any files and subdirectories in current directory, which have a name comprising of 3 characters, except the ones starting with a dot.

Bash – Intermediate

124: Write a simple script that will check the numeric UID of the user executing it, will display a message and then will exit, if the user is not root.
Answer:
#!/bin/bash

if (($(id -u) = 0))
then
  echo "Hello root"
else
  echo "You must login as root to execute this script!"
  exit 10
fi

exit

125: Construct a bash shell pattern to match any alphanumeric string ending with exactly one digit.
Answer:
*([a-zA-Z0-9])[a-za-Z][0-9]

126: Write a command that lists the filenames that match the pattern *Name#_##* exactly.
Answer:
echo Name[0-9]_[0-9][0-9]

127: Write a command to get the list of all directory entries (files & subdirectories) that starts with . (dot), except . (dot) and .. (double dot)
Answer:
echo .[!.]*

128: You must check if a certain file exists on your system and if you have read access to it. Which syntax will you use?
Answer:
if [[-f filename && -r filename]]
then
echo "filename exists and it's readable"
else
echo "filename does not exist or is not readable"
fi

129: Consider the following snippet:
mail user << end
Hello,
Please check the last entries logged from that program in $(hostname):
$(tail -10 /var/opt/application/logfile)
EOF
end
What is the message to be sent to the user?
Answer:
Hello,
Please check the last entries logged from that program in system's_hostname:
(the last 10 lines from the /var/opt/application/logfile)
EOF

130: What happens when you run this loop?
while read line
do
 echo $line
done < datafile

Answer:
This code reads the contents of datafile, line by line, and processes (here just displays) each line. It will finish when it reaches the end of file.

131: What happens when you run this loop?
while read line < datafile
do
 echo $line
done
Answer:
It is an infinite loop. Each iteration opens the datafile, reads only the first line, processes it (just displays it), and is repeated over and over.

132: You should find the entry that defines user account dbuser1 from the passwd file.
grep 'dbuser1' /etc/passwd
Is the above command:
correct,
correct but not exact or sufficient, or
completely insufficient,
Why?
Answer:
It is correct, but it is not exact or sufficient. This command will display all lines which contain the string dbuser1 in any position, not only in the start of the line, and before the field separator (:). The command which will return only the line starting with dbuser1will be as follows:
grep '^dbuser1:' /etc/passwd

133: Use the correct syntax to display all lines from the file named datafile that ends with the string ing. (a literal dot).
Answer:
grep 'ing\.$' datafile

134: A configuration file of an application (or service) contains many lines that are commented out, and just two or three useful lines. How could you display only the essential (uncommented) data?
Answer:
grep '^[^#]' conf_file
or
grep -v '^#' conf_file

135: How can the shell pass variables into *awk*?
Answer:
Using the *-v* option of *awk* and the reserved word *ENVIRON* of the *awk* inside the *awk* statement. e.g.:
var1="Some data"
awk -v Data="$var1" 'awk statement <'
awk syntax using an existing exported variable:
ENVIRON["var"]

136: True or False: When input is provided to *awk*, *awk* will process every record.
Answer:
TRUE

137: True or False: All unquoted strings are treated as variables, keywords or functions in *awk* statements.
Answer:

TRUE

138: You have a simple (text) contacts file, containing lines in the following format:
name country
There is also a file for each country, each containing a different message.
How could you display the different file for each country, merged after each entry which contains that country?
Answer:
Create a file containing a *sed* function matching each country and inserting the corresponding file into the output. For example:
/USA/r usa_file
/Australia/r australia_file
then, use the following command:
sed -f functions_file contacts_file

139: True or False: In bash shell the array variables can be multi-dimensional.
Answer:
FALSE

140: How could you display the entire contents of an array variable?
Answer:
echo ${array[*]}

141: How could you get the length (the total number of elements) of an array?
Answer:
echo ${#array[*]}

142: How could you initialize an array?
Answer:
set -A array value0 value1 <.

143: True or False: Array variables cannot be environment variables.
Answer:
TRUE

144: Is it possible to define a variable with local scope inside a function?
Answer:
Yes. If a variable is declared inside a function using the *declare* command or *typeset*, it exists only inside that function and is unset when function returns.

145: If you call a function using the syntax:
functionname /*
what will be the function's arguments (if any)?
Answer:
All the files & subdirectories under /, except dot files.

146: Is there any way to avoid overwriting the file when the following redirection syntax is used?
command > filename
Answer:
The shell option ***noclobber*** can be set to avoid overwriting the file.

147: Explain the following syntax:
command 2>&1 > /dev/null
Answer:

It redirects the *stderr* stream to file descriptor 1, that is, to the *stdout*, and then also redirects *stdout* to the special file /dev/null, discarding both, output and errors.

148: What is the result of the command?
kill $$
Answer:
It kills (terminates) the current process.

149: Why is it preferable to use the TERM signal (-15) instead of the KILL signal (-9) in order to stop the execution of a process?
Answer:
The TERM signal "says" to the process to start its normal termination procedure, so it is a safe way to terminate processes, closing their open files and releasing the resources. The KILL signal just "shoots" the process, so that, if there were open file descriptors, they remain open.

150: Is it possible to change the default behavior of the shell when it receives a certain signal?
Answer:
Yes, using the trap command. But not all signals are 'trapable', e.g., the KILL signal is not a trapable signal.

151: What is the meaning of $0 for an *awk* statement? What is the meaning of variables $1, $2/ .... for the *awk*?
Answer:
awk reads each line of input as *input record*, and splits each record in a set of numbered fields, in which the first field is *$1*, the second field is *$2*, and so on. The separator character used in this process is the value of *awk* special variable *FS*. The *$0* represents the entire

record.

152: Is it possible to define some actions to be performed before the processing of the input lines by the *awk* command?
Answer:
Yes, it is possible by using the reserved word *BEGIN* and putting the actions inside a block {}.

153: Select all of the following that apply to bash shell variables. Explain all that do not apply:
  a) Bash variables are untyped, by default.
  b) Although bash variables are basically treated as strings, the bash shell permits integer operations and comparisons on variables.
  c) All variables defined in a process (or shell) are local or private variables, that is, they are known only to that process.
  d) The variable names can contain any character, including special characters.

Answer:
Options a) and b) apply to bash shell variables.
Option c) does not apply. If variables have not been exported, yes, they are of local scope/ otherwise are "inherited" from any subprocess.
Option d) does not apply. The variables names can contain only alphanumerical characters and underscores, and the first character could not be a digit.

154: True or False: A script invoked from the command line can export variables back to its parent shell.
Answer:

FALSE

155: Write the echo command which will display the following line, using " (double quotes):
Some of Bash shell's special characters are: $, #, <, <<, >, >>, \, ', ", `, { }

Answer:
echo "Some of Bash shell's special characters are: \$, #, <, <<, >, >>, \\, ', \", \`, \{, \}"

156: How could you define your primary prompt to reflect the login name, the "at" sign, the system's hostname and the current working directory?

Answer:
PS1="\u@\h \w >"

157: How can you set the value of a variable to the contents of a file?

Answer:
  a) *variable=`cat file1`* (using command substitution with *cat*, thus with slower execution than the next one)
  b) *variable=`<file1`* (using command substitution with redirection)

158: Which are the differences between the two forms of command substitution, $(cmd) and `cmd`?

Answer:
  a) The newer form *$(cmd)* permits nesting, e.g.,
  count=$(wc -w $(ls -l | awk '{print $9}'))
  b) The two forms treat differently the double backslashes:
  echo `echo \\` will display an empty line, but

echo $(echo \ \) will display one \.

159: Describe the *and list* execution.
Answer:
An *and* list is a way of chaining together commands. The syntax is:
command 1 && command 2 && < command -n
Each command is executed in turn, provided the previous one has given an exit value of true. At the first false return value, the chain terminates and the remaining commands do not get executed.

160: Bash shell (version 4.2) permits representing and displaying characters in foreign alphabets. How? Give an example displaying the mathematical symbol PI.
Answer:
Bash supports the Unicode escape \u and \U. The command:
echo -e '\u220F'
displays the PI (π).

161: Give the output of the next code snippet:
a=5
let "val = a<6?1:2"
echo $val
let a++
let "val = a<6?2:3"
echo $val
Answer:
1   (from the first *echo*)
3   (from the second *echo*)

162: The permissions on a directory /mydir are rw-r---- and you are the owner of this directory. Can you display the contents of

/mydir? Can you change directory to /mydir? Can you create a new file under /mydir? Can you read the contents of a file contained in /mydir?

Answer:

Without the execute permission, you can change your current working directory to that directory, but you cannot use a trailing / (like in /mydir/) in any way. So, you can only execute the ls command to display the contents of this directory, but not ls -l, so it is not possible to get a long listing of this directory. You cannot execute a command like cat /mydir/file1, so it's impossible to access any file under the /mydir, regardless of its permissions, and it is also not possible to create a file there, since the syntax /mydir/ is not permitted.

163: Which are the two valid syntax forms to declare a function?

Answer:

   a) *function function_name {*
      commands
      }

   b) *function_name() {*
      commands
      }

164: Correct the following function's declaration.

holder() { echo "Press Return to continue<." ; read dummy }

Answer:

holder() { echo (Press Return to continue<.(; read dummy ; }   # missing semicolon before }

165: What does the += operator perform?

Answer:

In a numerical context, integer arithmetic (*let var+=1*)
In a string context, string concatenation (*string+=value*)

This page is intentionally left blank

Bash - Advanced

166: What kind of problems would occur if you define a function named *ls*?
Answer:
The function preempts or overrides the *ls* command.

167: Define a function named *pause_until_return*, to pause the execution of the script until the user presses the return key.
Answer:
function pause_until_return () {
echo (Press RETURN to continue <.(
read dummy
}

168: How can you create a functions library and what are the advantages of such a library?
Answer:
You can create a functions "library" file, that is, a file that contains functions declarations and common variables definitions, and then 'source' that "library file" from any script that needs to call any of these functions:
#!/bin/bash

.   */path_to_library/library_file #mind the dot (.)*
The advantages of using the function libraries are:
  a) Reduces the size of shell script files
  b) Easier updates. If a function library file is used by many scripts and the contents of the function file are modified, the updated version is immediately available to all scripts that call that function.

169: Is it permissible to use recursive functions (functions that call themselves)?
Answer:
Yes, but you must be careful so that not to start a kind of "infinite loop".

170: The following code snippet uses a file descriptor in order to create a file:
exec 3> /tmp/newfile
echo -u3 "First line <."
echot -u3 "Second line <"
exec 3>&-

The following code snippet creates the same exact file:
echo "First line <" > /tmp/newfile
echo "Second line ...." >> /tmp/newfile

But there is an important difference in the way of functioning of the above snippets. Could you explain it?
Answer:
The first snippet opens the *newfile* once, with the *exec 3>*, and then the file remains open until the execution of the second *exec*.
In the second snippet, the file is opened first time during the first *echo* command, then closes, then is opened again when the second *echo* starts, and then is closed again. This could be an important issue from performance's perspective, if this syntax will be used many times (e.g., inside a loop)

171: If you should use an interactive command (like *sftp*) in a script , what could you use in order to automate this function (without user interaction)?
Answer:

The so called "here" document

172: What is the output of the following?
netstat -rn | awk '/^def/ {print "Default gateway is ", $2}'
Answer:
The string "Default gateway is " followed by the IP Address of the defined default gateway.

173: What is the output of the following command?
*awk -F: '{BEGIN {OFS="=="} ; $2 = "****"; print NR "\t" $0}' /etc/passwd*
Answer:
The numbered lines of /etc/passwd, where the password field has been replaced by the string "****" and the separator ":" by the "==".

174: Explain the following pipeline.
grep bash file1 | diff file2 -
Answer:
The hyphen (-) is used to pipe stdout from the second command to other commands. Here, the pipeline compares the lines which contain the string "bash" from file1, to the entire contents of file2.

175: How could you declare an associative array?
Answer:
declare -A assoc

176: Which is the syntax which returns (expands to) the indexes in an array ARRAY?
Answer:
${!ARRAY[@]}
or

${!ARRAY[*]}

177: What is the built-in *mapfile* command used for?
Answer:
The *mapfile* builtin command is used to assign lines of standard input (and from a file with redirection) to an array defined by an argument, each line in a separate element. If no array is given in the command line, the default array name is *MAPFILE*. The target array must be an integer indexed array (not an associative one).

178: Write an equivalent but shorter form of the following *if* structure, without using *if*.
if [[$# -eq 0]]
then
    dirpath=$(pwd)
else
    dirpath=$@
fi
Answer:
[[$# -eq 0]] && dirpath=$(pwd) || dirpath=$@

179: Give the output of the next snippet and explain it:
a='$val1'
val1='$val2'
val2=newval
echo $a
eval echo $a
eval eval echo $a
Answer:
    a) a) *$val1* (first *echo*: single quotes do not permit any substitution)

b) b) *$val2* (second *echo - eval:* the invocation of *eval* forces a reevaluation of its arguments, so the arg *$a* is replaced by the value of a, that is, *$val1*; then *$val1* is replaced by the value of val1, that is, *$val2*)

c) *newval* (last line: The second invocation of *eval*, causes another re-evaluation of its argument, which is *$val2*, thus, replacing it with the value of val2, *newval*.)

180: Set the positional parameters to a string then unset the positional parameters and then set them again to their original values.

Answer:

new_positionals="Another string to be assigned to the positional parameters word by word"
orig_args=$@
echo $@   # Displays the current positionals params
set -- $new_positionals
echo $@   # Displays the contents of new_positionals
set --
echo $@   # Displays an empty line
set -- $orig_args
echo $@   # Displays the original args

181: The *rm* command just unlinks the file (inode) from the data blocks. To properly delete a file, it is required to overwrite the blocks occupied by the file. Create a script to securely delete the files passed to it as arguments.

Answer:
for i
do

       dd if=/dev/null of="$i" bs=1024 count=`expt 1 + `stat "$i" | grep 'Size:' | awk '{print $2}'` / 1024`
done

182: Assuming there is a defined array named *Array*, what does this *for* loop do?

```
for i in ${!Array[@]}
do
  echo ${Array[i]}
done
```

Answer:
It displays all the elements in *Array*. The notation *${!array[@]}* expands to all the indices of the *array*.

183: What is the impact of using the terminator characters *;;&* and *;&* in a *case* structure?

Answer:
The *;;&* terminator continues to the next pattern test.
The *;&* terminator executes the next statement even with a dummy pattern, that is, it executes the next statement even if the value does not match the pattern, so it's somewhat less useful and should be used with care.

184: Write the output of the following case, assuming that 1) $1 equals to a, and 2) $1 equals to 5:

```
case "$1" in
  [[:print:]] ) echo "$1 is a printable character.";;&
  [[:alnum:]] ) echo "$1 is an alpha/numeric character.";;&
  [[:alpha:]] ) echo "$1 is an alphabetic character.";;&
  [[:lower:]] ) echo "$1 is a lowercase alphabetic character.";;&
  [[:digit:]] ) echo "$1 is an numeric character.";&
```

@@%%*   )   echo "Dummy";;
esac

Answer:

a)   *a is a printable character.*
   a is an alpha/numeric character.
   a is an alphabetic character.
   a is a lowercase alphabetic character.
b) *5 is a printable character.*
   5 is an alpha/numeric character.
   5 is an numeric character.
   Dummy

185: Name two ways to set an array to the contents of a text file.
Answer:

a) declare -a ARRAY
 # Link filedescriptor 10 with stdin
exec 10<&0
exec < logfile
let count=0

while read LINE
do
   ARRAY[$count]=$LINE
   ((count++))
done
b) ARRAY=(`cat logfile `)

186: Name a limitation of *getopts* bash built-in.
Answer:

The *getopts* built-in does not support long option names with the double-dash prefix. It only supports single-character options.

187: Debug the following script excerpt:
number=1

while ["$number" < 5]
do
 echo -n "$number "
 let "number += 1"
done

Answer:
Should be:
number=1
while ["$number" -lt 5]
do
 echo -n "$number "
 let "number += 1"
done

188: Debug the following script excerpt:
function add_args ()
{
 echo "Adding two numbers"
 let "sumval = $1 + $2"
 echo $sumval
}

num1=42
num2=11
echo "Sum of $num1 and $num2 = $(add2 $num1 $num2)"

Answer:
function add_args ()
{

```
# echo "Adding two numbers"
# The output of this function is captured, and the two echo
# commands concatenate.
  let "sumval = $1 + $2"
  echo $sumval
}


num1=42
num2=11
echo "Sum of $num1 and $num2 = $(add2 $num1 $num2)"
```

189: Write a script that replaces every occurrence of a pattern with another in a given file. The script receives 3 arguments: pattern_to_be_replaced substitution_pattern filename
Answer:

```
#!/bin/bash

if [ $# -ne 3 ]
then
  echo "Usage: `basename $0` old-pattern new-pattern filename"
  exit 70
fi

old_p=$1
subst_p=$2

if [ -f "$3" ]
then
  filename=$3
else
  echo "File \"$3\" does not exist."
```

exit 70
fi

sed -e "s/$old_p/$subst_p/g" $filename

190: Create a function that capitalizes the first character of its string arguments.
Answer:
```
capital_char ()
{
  org_string="$@"
  for str in $@
  do
   firstchar=${str:0:1}
   rest_string=${str:1}
   FirstChar=`echo "$firstchar" | tr a-z A-Z`
   cap_string=${cap_string}" "$FirstChar$rest_string")
  done
}
```

191: What does the following code snippet do?
```
declare -A files
find . -type f -exec sha1sum {} + | while read -r sum fname
do
  if [[ ${files[$sum]} ]]
  then
   printf 'rm -- "%s" '
  else
   files[$sum]="$fname"
  fi
done > duplics
```

Answer:
It checks for duplicate files using a hash table (associative array) indexed with the SHA sum of the files in the current directory. sha1sum computes and checks SHA1 message digest. It prints or checks SHA1 (160-bit) checksums. This list passes through the while read loop to variables sum and fname. Then the script checks if there is already an element associated with the index $sum in the array files. If so, it is a duplicate file, and displays an "rm" message. Otherwise, the filename is added to the array files as a new element associated with the index $sum.

192: Describe the functionality of the following script:
#!/bin/bash

RESULT=mycgi.pl
(
cat << 'EOF'
#!/bin/perl

foreach $dir (split /:/, $ENV{PATH}) {
    echo "$dir\n";
}

EOF
) > $RESULT

Answer:
This script creates a perl script named *mycgi.pl*. The whole perl script is contained in here document. The end mark of here document (EOF) is enclosed in backquotes, thus disabling parameter substitution, so all lines in here document are treated and output as literal text.

193: Explain the next code snippet:
t=traffic
traffic=intolerable
echo "\"traffic\" = $traffic"
echo -n "dereferenced \"t\" = "
eval echo \$$t

t=traffic
traffic=unbelievable
unbelievable=intolerable
echo "Changing value of \"traffic\" to $traffic."
echo "\"traffic\" now is $traffic"
echo -n "dereferenced \"t\" now is"
eval echo \$$t

Answer:
The use of *\$$variable* in conjunction with *eval* means *indirect reference - dereference*. First $ is escaped and pasted on to the value of *var*. Variable t holds the name of another variable, and in second block, this variable (traffic) holds the value of another variable. The output produced by this snippet is:
"traffic"=intolerable
dereferenced "t"=intolerable

Changing value of "traffic" to unbelievable.
"traffic" now is unbelievable
dereferenced "t" now is intolerable

194: Which is the modern indirect reference form that is equivalent to the old one (*eval var1=\$$var2*)?
Answer:
${!variable}

eval var1=\$$var2 <=> var1=${!var2}

195: Explain this code snippet:
coproc { cat datafile; sleep 2; }

while read -u ${COPROC[0]} record
do
  echo "$record" | cut -c2-
done

kill $COPROC_PID

Answer:
The *coproc* builtin enables two parallel processes to communicate and interact. This coprocess communicates with the while read loop. *${COPROC[0]}* is the file descriptor of the coprocess. So, the while-read loop reads file datafile line by line, and removes the first character of each line from the output. At the end, when there is no longer need of the coprocess, it kills its *PID ($COPROC_PID)*.

196: The next excerpt does not achieve to set the 3 variables (*var1, var2, var3*). Explain.
var1=5
var2=6
var3=7

coproc echo "five six seven"
while read -u ${COPROC[0]} var1 var2 var3;
do
  echo "Inside while-read loop: ";
  echo "a = $a"; echo "b = $b"; echo "c = $c"
  echo "coproc file descriptor: ${COPROC[0]}"

done
echo "Outside while-read loop: ";
echo "a = $a"; echo "b = $b"; echo "c = $c"
echo "coproc file descriptor: ${COPROC[0]}"

Answer:

Inside the loop, everything is OK. The output will be:

Inside while-read loop:

a = five

b = six

c = seven

coproc file descriptor: something

But because this loop runs in a subshell, these values do not remain. So, the output of the three *echo* commands will be:

a=

b=

c=

The coprocess is still running, but the values are lost.

197: Write a script that recognizes and handles only the command options -*l* (followed by a value) and -*m* in any order. An invalid option will cause the script to terminate with an error, displaying the invalid option.

Answer:

#!/bin/bash

 # Usage: script [-l -m]
while getopts :l:m flag
do
 case $flag in
 l)   echo "Option has $OPTAGR as its value" ;;
 m) echo "Option -m received";;

*) echo "Invalid option $OPTARG";;
done

198: Give an example of downloading a URL using Bash shell.
Answer:
exec 3<>/dev/tcp/www.net.cn/80
echo -e "GET / HTTP/1.0\n" >&3
cat <&3
When executing a command on a /dev/tcp/$host/$port pseudo-device file, Bash opens a TCP connection to the associated *socket*. So it is possible to issue a HTTP GET.

199: Write the code to return a randomly selected index of an array (integer indexed), selecting a random element of the array.
Answer:
Array=(`ls -a`)   # Initialize an array
R_INDEX=$(($RANDOM%${#Array[@]}))   #${Array[@]} returns the lentgh of Array
 # $RANDOM%${#Array[@]} returns random integer between 1 and lentgh of array
R-ELEM=${Array[$R_INDEX]}

echo "Randomly selected element is $R_ELEM with index number $R_INDEX"

200: Write a snippet to return a randomly selected string index of an associative array and the element associated with this index.
Answer:
declare -A ass_array
ass_array[John]="john.k@domain1.com"

ass_array[Chris]="chris.sm@hotmail.com"
ass_array[Angela]="angela.st@domain5.com"

indices=(${!ass_array[*]})
count=${#indices[@]}
r_index_pos=$(($RANDOM%${#indices[@]}))
r_index=${indices[$r_index_pos]}
r_element=${ass_array[$r_index]}

echo "Randomly selected element is $r_element with index $r_index"

Q201: Name the obvious advantage of an *and list*.
Answer:
They can effectively replace complex *if/then* and/or *case* structures.

This page is intentionally left blank

HR Questions

Review these typical interview questions and think about how you would answer them. Read the answers listed; you will find best possible answers along with strategies and suggestions.

1: Tell me about yourself?
Answer:
The most often asked question in interviews. You need to have a short statement prepared in your mind. Keep your answer to one or two minutes. Don't ramble. Be careful that it does not sound rehearsed. Limit it to work-related items unless instructed otherwise. Talk about things you have done and jobs you have held that relate to the position you are interviewing for. Start with the item farthest back and work up to the present (If you have a profile or personal statement(s) at the top of your CV use this as your starting point).

2: Why did you leave your last job?
Answer:
Stay positive regardless of the circumstances. Never refer to a major problem with management and never speak ill of supervisors, co- workers or the organization. If you do, you will be the one looking bad. Keep smiling and talk about leaving for a positive reason such as an opportunity, a chance to do something special or other forward- looking reasons.

3: What experience do you have in this field?
Answer:
Speak about specifics that relate to the position you are applying for. If you do not have specific experience, get as close as you can.

4: Do you consider yourself successful?
Answer:
You should always answer yes and briefly explain why. A good explanation is that you have set goals, and you have met some and are on track to achieve the others.

5: What do co-workers say about you?
Answer:
Be prepared with a quote or two from co-workers. Either a specific statement or a paraphrase will work. Bill Smith, a co-worker at Clarke Company/ always said I was the hardest worker's he had ever known. It should be as powerful as Bill having said it at the interview herself.

6: What do you know about this organization?
Answer:
This question is one reason to do some research on the organization before the interview. Research the company's products, size, reputation, Image, goals, problems, management style, skills, History and philosophy. Be informed and interested. Find out where they have been and where they are going. What are the current issues and who are the major players?

7: What have you done to improve your knowledge in the last year?
Answer:
Try to include improvement activities that relate to the job. A wide variety of activities can be mentioned as positive self-improvement. Have some good ones handy to mention.

8: Are you applying for other jobs?
Answer:
Be honest but do not spend a lot of time in this area. Keep the focus on this job and what you can do for this organization. Anything else is a distraction.

9: Why do you want to work for this organization?

Answer:

This may take some thought and certainly, should be based on the research you have done on the organization. Sincerity is extremely important here and will easily be sensed. Relate it to your long-term career goals. Never talk about what you want; first talk about their Needs. You want to be part of an exciting forward-moving company. You can make a definite contribution to specific company goals.

10: Do you know anyone who works for us?
Answer:
Be aware of the policy on relatives working for the organization. This can affect your answer even though they asked about friends not relatives. Be careful to mention a friend only if they are well thought of.

11: What kind of salary do you need?
Answer:
A loaded question! A nasty little game that you will probably lose if you answer first. So, do not answer it. Instead, say something like/ that's a tough question. Can you tell me the range for this position? In most cases, the interviewer, taken off guard, will tell you. If not, say that it can depend on the details of the job. Then give a wide range.

12: Are you a team player?
Answer:
You are, of course, a team player. Be sure to have examples ready. Specifics that show you often perform for the good of the team rather than for yourself is good evidence of your team attitude. Do not brag; just say it in a matter-of-fact tone. This is a key point.

13: How long would you expect to work for us if hired?
Answer:
Specifics here are not good. Something like this should work:
I'd like it to be a long time. Or As long as we both feel I'm doing a good job.

14: Have you ever had to fire anyone? How did you feel about that?
Answer:
This is serious. Do not make light of it or in any way seem like you like to fire people. At the same time, you will do it when it is the right thing to do. When it comes to the organization versus the individual who has created a harmful situation, you will protect the organization. Remember firing is not the same as layoff or reduction in force.

15: What is your philosophy towards work?
Answer:
The interviewer is not looking for a long or flowery dissertation here. Do you have strong feelings that the job gets done? Yes. That's the type of answer that works best here. Keep it short and positive, showing a benefit to the organization.

16: If you had enough money to retire right now, would you?
Answer:
Answer yes if you would. But since you need to work, this is the type of work you prefer. Do not say yes if you do not mean it.

17: Have you ever been asked to leave a position?
Answer:
If you have not, say no. If you have, be honest, brief and avoid

saying negative things about the people or organization involved.

18: Explain how you would be an asset to this organization.
Answer:
You should be anxious for this question. It gives you a chance to highlight your best points as they relate to the position being discussed. Give a little advance thought to this relationship.

19: Why should we hire you?
Answer:
Point out how your assets meet what the organization needs. Also mention about your knowledge, experience, abilities, and skills. Never mention any other candidates to make a comparison.

20: Tell me about a suggestion you have made.
Answer:
Have a good one ready. Be sure and use a suggestion that was accepted and was then considered successful. One related to the type of work applied for is a real plus.

21: What irritates you about co-workers?
Answer:
This is a trap question. Think real hard but fail to come up with anything that irritates you. A short statement that you seem to get along with folks is great.

22: What is your greatest strength?
Answer:
Numerous answers are good, just stay positive. A few good examples: Your ability to prioritize, Your problem-solving skills, Your ability to work under pressure, Your ability to focus on

projects, Your professional expertise, Your leadership skills, Your positive attitude

23: Tell me about your dream job or what are you looking for in a job?
Answer:
Stay away from a specific job. You cannot win. If you say the job you are contending for is it, you strain credibility. If you say another job is it, you plant the suspicion that you will be dissatisfied with this position if hired. The best is to stay genetic and say something like: A job where I love the work, like the people, can contribute and can't wait to get to work.

24: Why do you think you would do well at this job?
Answer:
Give several reasons and include skills, experience and interest.

25: What do you find the most attractive about this position (Least attractive)?
Answer:
   a) List a couple of attractive factors such as the responsibility the post offers and the opportunity to work with experienced teams that have a reputation for innovation and creativity.
   b) Say you'd need more information and time before being able to make a judgment on any unattractive aspects.

26: What kind of person would you refuse to work with?
Answer:
Do not be trivial. It would take disloyalty to the organization, violence or lawbreaking to get you to object. Minor objections will

label you as a whiner.

27: What is more important to you: the money or the work?
Answer:
Money is always important, but the work is the most important. There is no better answer.

28: What would your previous supervisor say your strongest point is?
Answer:
There are numerous good possibilities:
Loyalty, Energy, Positive attitude, Leadership, Team player, Expertise, Initiative, Patience, Hard work, Creativity, Problem solver.

29: Tell me about a problem you had with a supervisor.
Answer:
Biggest trap of all! This is a test to see if you will speak ill of your boss. If you fall for it and tell about a problem with a former boss, you may well below the interview right there. Stay positive and develop a poor memory about any trouble with a supervisor.

30: What has disappointed you about a job?
Answer:
Don't get trivial or negative. Safe areas are few but can include: Not enough of a challenge. You were laid off in a reduction Company did not win a contract, which would have given you more responsibility.

31: Tell me about your ability to work under pressure.
Answer:

You may say that you thrive under certain types of pressure. Give an example that relates to the type of position applied for.

32: Do your skills match this job or another job more closely?
Answer:
Probably this one! Do not give fuel to the suspicion that you may want another job more than this one.

33: What motivates you to do your best on the job?
Answer:
This is a personal trait that only you can say, but good examples are: Challenge, Achievement, and Recognition.

34: Are you willing to work overtime? Nights? Weekends?
Answer:
This is up to you. Be totally honest.

35: How would you know you were successful on this job?
Answer:
Several ways are good measures:
You set high standards for yourself and meet them. Your outcomes are a success. Your boss tells you that you are successful and doing a great job.

36: Would you be willing to relocate if required?
Answer:
You should be clear on this with your family prior to the interview if you think there is a chance it may come up. Do not say yes just to get the job if the real answer is no. This can create a lot of problems later on in your career. Be honest at this point. This will save you from future grief.

37: Are you willing to put the interests of the organization ahead of your own?
Answer:
This is a straight loyalty and dedication question. Do not worry about the deep ethical and philosophical implications. Just say yes.

38: Describe your management style.
Answer:
Try to avoid labels. Some of the more common labels, like progressive, salesman or consensus, can have several meanings or descriptions depending on which management expert you listen to. The situational style is safe, because it says you will manage according to the situation, instead of one size fits all.

39: What have you learned from mistakes on the job?
Answer:
Here you have to come up with something or you strain credibility. Make it small, well intentioned mistake with a positive lesson learned. An example would be, working too far ahead of colleagues on a project and thus throwing coordination off.

40: Do you have any blind spots?
Answer:
Trick question! If you know about blind spots, they are no longer blind spots. Do not reveal any personal areas of concern here. Let them do their own discovery on your bad points. Do not hand it to them.

41: If you were hiring a person for this job, what would you look for?

Answer:
Be careful to mention traits that are needed and that you have.

42: Do you think you are overqualified for this position?
Answer:
Regardless of your qualifications, state that you are very well qualified for the position you've been interviewed for.

43: How do you propose to compensate for your lack of experience?
Answer:
First, if you have experience that the interviewer does not know about, bring that up: Then, point out (if true) that you are a hard working quick learner.

44: What qualities do you look for in a boss?
Answer:
Be generic and positive. Safe qualities are knowledgeable, a sense of humor, fair, loyal to subordinates and holder of high standards. All bosses think they have these traits.

45: Tell me about a time when you helped resolve a dispute between others.
Answer:
Pick a specific incident. Concentrate on your problem solving technique and not the dispute you settled.

46: What position do you prefer on a team working on a project?
Answer:
Be honest. If you are comfortable in different roles, point that out.

47: Describe your work ethic.
Answer:
Emphasize benefits to the organization. Things like, determination to get the job done and work hard but enjoy your work are good.

48: What has been your biggest professional disappointment?
Answer:
Be sure that you refer to something that was beyond your control. Show acceptance and no negative feelings.

49: Tell me about the most fun you have had on the job.
Answer:
Talk about having fun by accomplishing something for the organization.

50: What would you do for us? (What can you do for us that someone else can't?)
a) Relate past experiences that represent success in Working for your previous employer.
b) Talk about your fresh perspective and the relevant experience you can bring to the company.
c) Highlight your track record of providing creative, Workable solutions.

51: Do you have any questions for me?
Answer:
Always have some questions prepared. Questions prepared where you will be an asset to the organization are good. How soon will I be able to be productive? What type of projects will I be able to assist on?

And Finally Good Luck!

INDEX

UNIX Shell Programming Questions

C Shell - Beginner

1: What must you do before you are able to run your new script for the first time by its name or with an alias?

2: The following command is included in the .login script of a user:

3: If the condition *If (-r filename)* fails (returns false), what are the possible reasons?

4: Which is the difference between the next two statements?

5: Given the code snippet:

6: What will the output of the following commands be? Explain.

7: What does the command *rehash* do?

8: How could you ensure that a script will be run in csh?

9: Given that *script1* is an executable C shell script situated in directory */home/myhomedir/project1/data/dir1*, use three ways to run it, explaining the pros and cons.

10: What will be the value of the *sixrem* variable, after executing this command?

11: Name two ways to obtain the length of a string, giving a simple example for each one.

12: Create a script that displays a list of regular files from the current directory.

13: Describe in short the word completion feature of the tcsh shell.

14: In tcsh, how are the remaining choices (if any) listed whenever the word completion fails?

15: In tcsh, how do you disable filename substitution?

16: Compare the *sched* tcsh built-in command with the UNIX/Linux *at* command.

17: Schedule a prompt change at 10:55 as a reminder for an oncoming event.

18: What is the impact of *-f* option in the first line of a csh script?

19: How can you start a job in the background, and then terminate your login session, without terminating the background job?

20: Which is the difference between

21: Display the first and last arguments of a script, regardless of the number of arguments, and without a loop.

22: Describe the two ways to set the search path in csh.

23: Create a tar archive into */home/user1/myarch.tar*, including all files ending in *.c, .h, .l, .y,.o* and *.cc* and also the *Makefile* from two directories, ~/dir1 and ~/dir2.

24: Your script must be executed with exactly two arguments, otherwise would be terminated. Write a code to implement these checks.

25: Write a pipeline that reads from the j-th line up to the k-th line of a text file, without using *awk*.

C Shell - Intermediate

26: Explain the following commands:

27: How could you move cursor to specified coordinates on screen? (tcsh)

28: What is the result of this loop?

29: Assuming there is a label cleanup somewhere in a script, explain the command *onintr cleanup*

30: Is there a way to repeat a command for a predefined number of times, without using a counter-controlled loop?

31: csh and tcsh both support the filename & command completion feature. But the feature works differently in csh than in tcsh. Name the differences.

32: Name the special login files for csh & tcsh in the order used by each shell.

33: What do the following lines do? Explain the differences.

34: You can run a script by its name, using an alias or using source. Explain the differences in using each of the three methods. When is it suitable to use each method?

35: How could you override a defined alias? Give a simple example.

36: You plan to write a script that will process the file passed to it as the only argument on the command line. So, your script must accept at least one argument and this single or first argument must be an existing file. Write the necessary checks, displaying the appropriate messages.

37: Write a code excerpt that processes (here, just displays) the elements of an array, from the first one to the last one.

38: Complete the last *echo* command with a descriptive message in the following script. In other words, explain the value of *pct* variable.

39: Extract just the mode of a given file, using two different ways.

40: Which is the output of the following excerpt?

41: Find the position of a substring in a given string. Display a message if the string does not contain this substring.

42: Change the case of a string.

43: Assume that in a script the value of a variable *limt* becomes equal to 92.1. Display the message:

44: Suppose a script contains the following snippet:

45: Create a script that converts the filenames from current directory to lower case letters.

46: Name some basic differences between csh and tcsh.

47: Compare the tcsh shell variables *correct* and *autocorrect*.

48: What is the purpose of the special alias *shell*?

49: Which is the method to bind the keys to the standard *vi* or *emacs* bindings?

50: Which is the purpose of shell's variable *color*?

51: Set your prompt to display *username@hostname: pwd>*

52: How can you start (from shell prompt) 2 commands "in the background", ensuring that the second command will start after the completion of the first one?

53: Write a script to display a sorted listing of the unique words in a text file.

54: Display the value of your *PATH* variable with each path in a separate line.

55: Why the inclusion of a dot (.) in a search path is not a good practice?

56: Explain the logical expression @ $x = (\$n < 5 \;||\; 20 <= \$n)$ and then also write the negation of this expression.

57: Are there any differences between the next two commands? When is it suitable to use each one?

58: The creation of aliases in your *.cshrc* file does have a drawback: if you define many aliases in the *.cshrc* file, it will decelerate process activation. What would be a possible work around?

59: Explain this small script:

60: A script prompts the user to type in something, using the following syntax:

C Shell - Advanced

61: Fix the next switch statement, explaining your corrections:

62: Name some basic differences between bash and csh syntax and/or features.

63: Suggest a way to overcome lack of functions in C shells.

64: From /tmp directory, issue *(cd ; pwd) ; pwd*. Explain the performed actions and the output.

65: Write a code excerpt that prompts for a filename, reads the user input, checks if this is a regular file and if so, stores it in an array for further processing. The procedure must be repeated until the user hits the Enter key.

66: Use *awk* mathematical functions to calculate the area of a circle (area = PI*rad^2)

67: Use *awk* in order to split an entry from /etc/passwd file into an array, replacing the password field with the string "secret".

68: Explain the following snippet:

69: Name the available ways (with examples) to replace any occurrence of a substring with another substring in a string.

70: Write a snippet to categorize the files from a directory, based on their extension (for simplicity, take care only for *.c, .o, .txt,* and *.png* files). Create an array for each extension, containing the filenames. Finally, display the number of files for each extension.

71: Write a script that will display a menu of choices to the user. The menu should be displayed over and over, until the user will select the specific "exit" option. The script should give to the user the following options:

72: Create a script that will be run automatically when the user logs into the system, and send a mail message to the user, if the total number of aliases on his .cshrc file are greater than a threshold (let's say 40).

73: Display the filenames and permissions of each file in your current directory.

74: Create a script that creates a list of all file systems (mount points) on the current system and the current percent used.

75: Explain the following script and suggest any enhancements:

76: Assuming that script *myscript.csh* executes successfully, explain why the command:

77: In which case the following command would be useful?

78: Use the *bc* calculator in order to do a variable comparison involving floating-point numbers. Write your example as part of an *if* conditional statement.

79: Write a *while* loop using a floating-point comparison statement as the loop condition (and loop control).

80: There is no simple file reading facility in the C-shell. What could you use to tide this over?

81: Extract the n-th line of a text file and assign it in a variable.

82: Assuming that input_file is a text file with space-separated fields, what will be the value of *ncol* when the next command will be executed?

83: Find the minimum of the integer numbers that are stored in an array.

84: Explain the following block of commands:

85: The C shell provides one way to read a line:

86: Explain the following snippet:

87: Fix any syntax or logical error in the following script:

88: Explain this script:

89: Are there any differences between the next two commands?

90: Explain the following code block:

91: Suppose that you have a contacts file in the format (no headers line):

92: Which is the valid syntax of *getopt* command in a C shell?

93: Explain in short the following script:

94: Write a script which calculates the min, max and average of a set of floating-point numbers, stored in an array.

95: You have an input data file with a symmetrical schema (the same number of fields in each record) where the first line contains the headings of the fields. You want to extract the 3rd column (field) of the actual data records, that is, of each record except the headers line

(1st line) and any comment lines (assume that they begin with # or *). Give a solution and explain it in short.

96: Suppose that input_file is a tabular data file with an asymmetric schema, that is, each record (line) may have different number of fields, and that the first 3 lines describe the used schema. Explain the following excerpt:

97: Suppose you have a data file but its internal format does not remain consistent. You want to extract two columns from this file, but you don't know the order of the columns, only their headers: Name, and email.

Write the script that will achieve these tasks.

98: Create a script to read a textfile line by line, to the end of the file. Do not use *awk*.

99: Which is a limitation in options handling in C shells?

100: Rewrite the next script, using a more readable and clear logic:

Bash - Beginner

101: Consider the following message:

102: The *case* statement is useful for comparing the value of a variable against a list of possible matches. True or false?

103: You don't remember the correct option (switch) for *sort* command, in order to sort some entries in reverse order. What could you do?

104: The first line of a shell script is:

105: You need to find all files under your /home directory that were not accessed during last 10 days. What could you do?

106: How could you check if there are running *sshd* processes on your system?

107: What happens when you run the following command?

108: The next line is the beginning of a conditional statement in a bash script:

109: A *for* loop requires an arguments list. This list can result from:

110: Given the following nested loops, which command would you use in place of command-to-process-file for the shell to execute the last cat command, if the test condition is met?

111: What would happen if the following command was in the .bash_profile of a user?

112: The value of a variable should be compared against 8 possible values (and/or patterns) and some commands, different for each possible value, should be run. Which is the structure that you would prefer for these checks?

113: What is the expected output from the following command?

114: How can you run a job in the background?

115: What is the action performed by the command *cd -*?

116: Which are the special meanings of character ~ for the bash shell?

117: Which is the difference between *variable5* and *$variable5*?

118: What is defined with the command *variable=value*, a local or an environment variable?

119: How can you find the bash shell version which is installed on your system?

120: What does the bash built-in variable *EDITOR* do?

121: What is the purpose of shell built-in variable *PATH*?

122: Is there any way to declare an integer variable in bash?

123: How would the shell interpret the command "*echo ??a*"?

Bash - Intermediate

124: Write a simple script that will check the numeric UID of the user executing it, will display a message and then will exit, if the user is not root.

125: Construct a bash shell pattern to match any alphanumeric string ending with exactly one digit.

UNIX Shell Programming Interview Questions You'll Most Likely Be Asked   115

126: Write a command that lists the filenames that match the pattern *Name#_##* exactly.

127: Write a command to get the list of all directory entries (files & subdirectories) that starts with . (dot), except . (dot) and .. (double dot)

128: You must check if a certain file exists on your system and if you have read access to it. Which syntax will you use?

129: Consider the following snippet:

130: What happens when you run this loop?

131: What happens when you run this loop?

132: You should find the entry that defines user account dbuser1 from the passwd file.

133: Use the correct syntax to display all lines from the file named datafile that ends with the string ing. (a literal dot).

134: A configuration file of an application (or service) contains many lines that are commented out, and just two or three useful lines. How could you display only the essential (uncommented) data?

135: How can the shell pass variables into *awk*?

136: True or False: When input is provided to *awk*, *awk* will process every record.

137: True or False: All unquoted strings are treated as variables, keywords or functions in *awk* statements.

138: You have a simple (text) contacts file, containing lines in the following format:

139: True or False: In bash shell the array variables can be multi-dimensional.

140: How could you display the entire contents of an array variable?

141: How could you get the length (the total number of elements) of an array?

142: How could you initialize an array?

143: True or False: Array variables cannot be environment variables.

144: Is it possible to define a variable with local scope inside a function?

145: If you call a function using the syntax:

146: Is there any way to avoid overwriting the file when the following redirection syntax is used?

147: Explain the following syntax:

148: What is the result of the command?

149: Why is it preferable to use the TERM signal (-15) instead of the KILL signal (-9) in order to stop the execution of a process?

150: Is it possible to change the default behavior of the shell when it receives a certain signal?

151: What is the meaning of *$0* for an *awk* statement? What is the meaning of variables *$1, $2/* …. for the *awk*?

152: Is it possible to define some actions to be performed before the processing of the input lines by the *awk* command?

153: Select all of the following that apply to bash shell variables. Explain all that do not apply:

154: True or False: A script invoked from the command line can export variables back to its parent shell.

155: Write the echo command which will display the following line, using " (double quotes):

156: How could you define your primary prompt to reflect the login name, the "at" sign, the system's hostname and the current working directory?

157: How can you set the value of a variable to the contents of a file?

158: Which are the differences between the two forms of command substitution, *$(cmd)* and `cmd`?

159: Describe the *and list* execution.

160: Bash shell (version 4.2) permits representing and displaying characters in foreign alphabets. How? Give an example displaying the mathematical symbol PI.

161: Give the output of the next code snippet:

162: The permissions on a directory /mydir are rw-r---- and you are the owner of this directory. Can you display the contents of /mydir? Can you change directory to /mydir? Can you create a new file under /mydir? Can you read the contents of a file contained in /mydir?

163: Which are the two valid syntax forms to declare a function?

164: Correct the following function's declaration.

165: What does the += operator perform?

Bash - Advanced

166: What kind of problems would occur if you define a function named *ls*?

167: Define a function named *pause_until_return*, to pause the execution of the script until the user presses the return key.

168: How can you create a functions library and what are the advantages of such a library?

169: Is it permissible to use recursive functions (functions that call themselves)?

170: The following code snippet uses a file descriptor in order to create a file:

171: If you should use an interactive command (like *sftp*) in a script, what could you use in order to automate this function (without user interaction)?

172: What is the output of the following?

173: What is the output of the following command?

174: Explain the following pipeline.

175: How could you declare an associative array?

176: Which is the syntax which returns (expands to) the indexes in an array ARRAY?

177: What is the built-in *mapfile* command used for?

178: Write an equivalent but shorter form of the following *if* structure, without using *if*.

179: Give the output of the next snippet and explain it:

180: Set the positional parameters to a string then unset the positional parameters and then set them again to their original values.

181: The *rm* command just unlinks the file (inode) from the data blocks. To properly delete a file, it is required to overwrite the blocks occupied by the file. Create a script to securely delete the files passed to it as arguments.

182: Assuming there is a defined array named *Array*, what does this *for* loop do?

183: What is the impact of using the terminator characters *;;&* and *;&* in a *case* structure?

184: Write the output of the following case, assuming that 1) $1 equals to a, and 2) $1 equals to 5:

185: Name two ways to set an array to the contents of a text file.

186: Name a limitation of *getopts* bash built-in.

187: Debug the following script excerpt:

188: Debug the following script excerpt:

189: Write a script that replaces every occurrence of a pattern with another in a given file. The script receives 3 arguments: *pattern_to_be_replaced substitution_pattern filename*

190: Create a function that capitalizes the first character of its string arguments.

191: What does the following code snippet do?

192: Describe the functionality of the following script:

193: Explain the next code snippet:

194: Which is the modern indirect reference form that is equivalent to the old one (*eval var1=\$$var2*)?

195: Explain this code snippet:

196: The next excerpt does not achieve to set the 3 variables (*var1, var2, var3*). Explain.

197: Write a script that recognizes and handles only the command options *-l* (followed by a value) and *-m* in any order. An invalid option will cause the script to terminate with an error, displaying the invalid option.

198: Give an example of downloading a URL using bash shell.

199: Write the code to return a randomly selected index of an array (integer indexed), selecting a random element of the array.

200: Write a snippet to return a randomly selected string index of an associative array and the element associated with this index.

201: Name the obvious advantage of an *and list*.

HR Questions

1: Tell me about yourself?
2: Why did you leave your last job?
3: What experience do you have in this field?
4: Do you consider yourself successful?
5: What do co-workers say about you?
6: What do you know about this organization?
7: What have you done to improve your knowledge in the last year?
8: Are you applying for other jobs?
9: Why do you want to work for this organization?
10: Do you know anyone who works for us?
11: What kind of salary do you need?
12: Are you a team player?
13: How long would you expect to work for us if hired?
14: Have you ever had to fire anyone? How did you feel about that?
15: What is your philosophy towards work?
16: If you had enough money to retire right now, would you?
17: Have you ever been asked to leave a position?
18: Explain how you would be an asset to this organization.
19: Why should we hire you?
20: Tell me about a suggestion you have made.
21: What irritates you about co-workers?
22: What is your greatest strength?
23: Tell me about your dream job or what are you looking for in a job?
24: Why do you think you would do well at this job?
25: What do you find the most attractive about this position? (Least attractive?)
26: What kind of person would you refuse to work with?
27: What is more important to you: the money or the work?
28: What would your previous supervisor say your strongest point is?
29: Tell me about a problem you had with a supervisor.
30: What has disappointed you about a job?
31: Tell me about your ability to work under pressure.
32: Do your skills match this job or another job more closely?
33: What motivates you to do your best on the job?
34: Are you willing to work overtime? Nights? Weekends?
35: How would you know you were successful on this job?

36: Would you be willing to relocate if required?
37: Are you willing to put the interests of the organization ahead of your own?
38: Describe your management style.
39: What have you learned from mistakes on the job?
40: Do you have any blind spots?
41: If you were hiring a person for this job, what would you look for?
42: Do you think you are overqualified for this position?
43: How do you propose to compensate for your lack of experience?
44: What qualities do you look for in a boss?
45: Tell me about a time when you helped resolve a dispute between others.
46: What position do you prefer on a team working on a project?
47: Describe your work ethic.
48: What has been your biggest professional disappointment?
49: Tell me about the most fun you have had on the job.
50: What would you do for us? (What can you do for us that someone else can't?)
51: Do you have any questions for me?

Some of the following titles might also be handy:
1: Oracle / PLSQL Interview Questions
2: ASP.NET Interview Questions
3: VB.NET Interview Questions
4: .NET Framework Interview Questions
5: C#.NET Interview Questions
6: OOPS Interview Questions
7: Core Java Interview Questions
8: JSP-Servlet Interview Questions
9: EJB (J2EE) Interview Questions
10: ADO.NET Interview Questions
11: SQL Server Interview Questions
12: C & C++ Interview Questions
13: 200 (HR) Interview Questions
14: JavaScript Interview Questions
15: JAVA/J2EE Interview Questions
16: Oracle DBA Interview Questions
17: XML Interview Questions
18: UNIX Shell Programming Interview Questions
19: PHP Interview Questions
20: J2ME Interview Questions
21: Hardware and Networking Interview Questions
22: Data Structures & Algorithms Interview Questions
23: Oracle E-Business Suite Interview Questions
24: UML Interview Questions
25: HTML, XHTML & CSS Interview Questions
26: JDBC Interview Questions
27: Hibernate, Springs & Struts Interview Questions
28: Linux Interview Questions

For complete list visit
www.vibrantpublishers.com